Ten Ways to Become a
Better Reader

1. Read	6. Read
2. Read	7. Read
3. Read	8. Read
4. Read	9. Read
5. Read	10. Read

Practical Advice from Real Teachers

Written by **Cindy Merrilees** and **Pamela Haack**

Foreword by Jim Trelease

Pictures by Mike Denman
Photographs by Peggy McAteer

We are forever grateful to

Robert Haack (for his inspiring slogan, "Ten Ways to Become a Better Reader"), Sherrill Hickman, Theresa Roman, Sandy Emery, Steve Lowe and our 1988-89 third grade classes for showing us the "magic."

CONTENTS

FOREWORD

By Jim Trelease
Author of *The New Read-Aloud Handbook*

As a former soldier, I've always felt the best people to write an Army manual on foxhole-digging would be privates and corporals. The worst authors for such a manual would be majors, colonels, and generals. Most of the latter cannot remember the last foxhole they dug.

And the same rule applies to "education" books like this one. Give me the observant teacher who has been in the trenches, the creative one struggling day in and day out with beginning or reluctant readers, the one with a limited income for supplies and materials, the one pressed for meaningful time in an over-crowded curriculum. When *this* kind of teacher exclaims, "Look what I have discovered! Here's a formula that works in my classroom again and again," it behooves you to sit up and listen.

Most parents and teachers pay only lip service to theories. What they most need and appreciate is practical advice. And that's the winning part of this book and its authors: two teachers from the trenches with simple, everyday help to create lifetime readers instead of just schooltime readers. The lifetime reader should be the objective of all teaching -- that is, the graduate who continues educating himself or herself throughout life. The schooltime reader, unfortunately, represents all too large a proportion of our alumni. These are the students who read only when someone *makes* them read, who never or seldom read for pleasure, and who stop reading on graduation day.

The question of how we produce one and not the other is the challenge of American education in the 1990s, a decade that began with no significant rise in student reading scores in nearly twenty-five years. Family shopping time rose, television viewing time increased, as did video games, but reading slumped. Why?

Two obvious answers are often overlooked because they are so simple. The first is that we humans (adults and children) are a pleasure-oriented species. We quickly and willingly gravitate to the things that bring us pleasure and avoid the things that bring us pain. We thus become more proficient and do better at the skills we enjoy and practice less those we don't enjoy.

Now couple that principle with the fact that reading is an accrued skill -- the more you read the better you get at it. The better you get at it, the more you like it; and the more you like reading, the more you read, ad infinitum. In other words, the only way to get from a basic fourth-grade reading level to an eighth-grade and then to a twelfth-grade level is to read a lot. But because of that pleasure principle, they won't read a lot if they hate it. And if we have learned anything over the last thirty years of programmed learning, it is how children learn to *hate* reading. Simply give them 1000 work sheets a school year, test them and grade them on every word, convince them that books are written not to be enjoyed but to be passed or failed, and you have a schooltime reader by fourth grade.

Some teachers -- the ones who through the decades have been most successful in producing lifetime readers -- have long known how to create a book environment and teaching ethic that is non-threatening and stress-free, that opens doors and invites the beginning reader inside. But it is through teachers like Cindy Merrilees and Pamela Haack that the numbers of such enlightened teachers will expand. As more and more educators (including principals, supervisors, and parents) finally concede that the old way has taught students HOW to read but failed to teach children to WANT to read, they turn to viable alternatives like this book.

Yes, the whole language movement and the literature-based curriculum coincide perfectly with an approach like this one. But more importantly, the developmental needs and desires of children dovetail with it. Children meet the concepts of reading, writing, and authors while at the same time learning long and short vowels, past-, present-, and future-tense verbs, and critical thinking skills but within a framework that is both meaningful and pleasurable.

INTRODUCTION

Do you feel pressured by teaching reading?
Do you feel that you don't have time for
all your reading groups every day?
Do you feel pressured when teaching
reading skills?
Do you have a hard time seeing the
connection between reading skills and
reading?
Do you feel that your students don't get
to read enough?

Do your students moan and groan when
you call their reading group?
Do your students hate reading groups?

Do YOU hate reading groups?

If you answered yes to any of the above questions, this book is for you!

We, the authors, answered yes to *all* the above questions and realized that
we had to do something about it. So we did!

Our first motivating experience was a Whole Language workshop held at
our school. The workshop gave us an overview of the Whole Language
movement in the United States and the opportunity to develop related
classroom activities.

Through trial and error, we have learned what works and what doesn't
work, and we continue to learn more every day. What we know for sure
is that our students LOVE reading and have developed the self-confidence
to become readers for life. Our students are addicted to reading—and so
are we!

Although the title of our book is *Ten Ways to Become a Better Reader*, there is really only one -- read! This book includes ideas and activities that helped us encourage our students to do just that.

It is our goal to spread the enthusiasm and love we have found in sharing books with our children. We were already dedicated teachers, but now our days are filled with magic—

- the magic in a child's eyes when she finishes her first "whole" book,

- the magic hug from the "class toughie" when a touching novel is finished,

- the magic you feel when a child tells you his mom cried when he read her a book for the first time,

- the magic sound of your whole class laughing at something you just read *together*,

- the magic you feel when your students beg for more reading time.

Give our ideas a try and share the

THE TRANSITION

BEFORE...

AFTER...

THE TRANSITION
FROM READING GROUPS TO WHOLE GROUP READING

The transition from reading groups to whole group reading is scary. It takes guts and the ability to rely on your own professionalism and creativity. As teachers, we have become so restricted and stifled by teacher's editions, level tests, and other accountability measures that we've lost the confidence to use our own ideas. Teachers know what works and what doesn't! Whole group reading works! It works because it builds confidence, motivates, and builds enough vocabulary to make walking dictionaries out of your students. It excites, stimulates imaginations, and fosters creativity to the point that reading becomes just plain FUN for the teacher and class.

Make the transition a comfortable one. These steps are just guidelines. Proceed at a pace that is comfortable for you.

Step 1. Experience whole group reading.

Remember, whole group reading is not "something extra." Your day is full enough. Take a day off from your regular schedule and give one of these ideas a try.

- Read a story from the basal, whole group, from beginning to end with no questions.

- Hold whole class reading on your floor.

- Read aloud to your class.

- Read a big book.

- Pass out copies of a poem and learn it with your students. (Bet they memorize it faster than you do!)

- Introduce your favorite author to the class.

- Make a class book.

TYPICAL MORNING BEFORE:

TYPICAL MORNING AFTER:

Step 2. Change your daily routine.

Your daily routine will need some changes. Make the changes gradually. Stick with what's comfortable.

- *Reading*
  Start your day by reading with your class. Spend an enjoyable 60-90 minutes of reading interaction with your students. (This is the time for reading big books, small books, or poems, writing books discovering authors, or reading aloud). Emphasize any skills you will be teaching during skill focus time. This helps students see how the skills relate to their reading. (For example, if you will be teaching "cause and effect" during skill focus time, point out examples of "cause and effect" in the story you are reading.)

- *Lesson Time*
  Use this time to teach language arts—not just for review or "busy work."

- *Skill Focus*
  Focus on the tested, accountable reading skills children discovered during whole group reading. (Be sure to refer to this time as "skill focus," not "reading" or even "reading skills." Let your students know that reading is reading! It is that wonderful time you spend together with books each morning.)

- *Independent and Group Activity*
  This is your chance for individual and small group assistance, conferencing, and informal assessment.

Step 3. Change Your Class Environment

- Get rid of your reading table! (If you can't get it out of your room, it makes a great plant stand!)

- Arrange your desks to clear a sizable floor area for little bottoms!

- Get creative with a reading corner!

- Boast about your students' accomplishments!

TEACHING STRATEGIES

TEACHING STRATEGIES

Dare to try something new. Begin with the technique that appeals to you most. As you and your class become comfortable with whole group reading, add more activities to your schedule.

BIG BOOKS

Big Books are a good starting point for making the transition from reading groups to whole group reading. The steps we suggest for using a Big Book should take about a week. (A detailed lesson plan appears on pages 18-20.)

Step 1. Pick a book you like. Teacher enthusiasm is necessary and yours will be contagious!

Step 2. Read the book to your students. You might want to spend time talking about the cover, title, author, copyright date, and dedication page or predicting the story from the cover. But once you start reading the story, don't stop until you get to the end. It is important to slide your hand or a pointer under the text as you read.

Step 3. Read the book a second time. This time, ask students to join in when they like. (You'll notice almost all students joining in on the predictable and repetitive parts.) Never put children on the spot. Let them read when they volunteer, but avoid calling on students who may not yet feel confident enough to read solo.

Step 4. After the second reading, talk about new words, interesting illustrations, story content, main idea, sequencing, fact and opinion, drawing conclusions, blends, or other reading skills that arise from the story. Be sure to emphasize the skills you will teach during skill focus time.

Step 5. Now divide the children into groups to reread the book. Experiment with various methods of grouping:

- individual volunteers
- girls/boys
- character parts (Stress reading words inside quotes.)
- tall kids/short kids
- small groups

SAMPLE BIG BOOK LESSON PLAN

Peanut Butter and Jelly by Joanne Nelson. Pictures by B. K. Taylor. Modern Curriculum Press, 1989.

Key: A=Activities   SF= Skills Focus   E=Evaluation and Assessment

MONDAY	TUESDAY	WEDNESDAY
- - - - Whole Group Reading: Peanut Butter and Jelly - - - -		
A: Read story to class. Discuss cover, title page, copyright.	A: Read story, asking students to join in. Discuss story content and illustrations.	A: Read story with students. Discuss story to assess understanding of story content and word meaning from context.
SF: No new skills introduced on first day of story.	SF: No new skills introduced.	SF: Rhyming words. Point out in story.

THURSDAY	FRIDAY
Whole Group Reading: Peanut Butter and Jelly	
A: Reading of story by small groups and	A: Reread story using a variation. individuals.

Enrichment activities. |
| SF: Review rhyming words.

E: Assess students' understanding of rhyming words through short poems. | |

DAY 1

Activities:

■ Talk about the book's cover, title, author, and illustrator.

■ Discuss the title page, and copyright.

■ Invite students to predict what the story might be about just from looking at the cover.

■ Read the book to your students *without* stopping.

■ Initiate an informal discussion about the story, taking time to let the children enjoy the illustrations.

Skills Focus:

■ It is best not to pull skills from the story the first day.

DAY 2

Activities:

■ Review content, author, illustrator, and copyright.

■ Reread the story to your students. Encourage them to join in.

■ Read the story *with* students. Discuss story content in depth. Ask literal and inferential questions. Sample questions for Peanut Butter and Jelly include the following.

- Who is telling this story?
- What kinds of foods does the narrator like to eat?
- Do you and the narrator have common tastes?
- Where does the story take place?
- Are any of these places similar to places in your neighborhood?
- Are there any other characters in the story?
- Would your pet act this way?
- What does your pet do while you are eating?
- What are some of your favorite foods?

DAY 3

Activities:

■ Read the story with your students. To assess students' reading abilities, ask individuals or small groups of students to read aloud.

Skills Focus--Rhyming Words:

■ Review rhyming words from the story, and list them on the chalkboard. Challenge students to think of other rhyming words and make individual lists.

Note: Skill Focus in the morning with big books is designed to introduce or reinforce skills in context. Later in the day, "teach" the same skill in lesson format.

DAY 4

Activities:

■ Reread the story, asking individual students to read each page aloud.

Skills Focus:

■ Review rhyming words. Encourage students to share their rhyming word lists orally.

Evaluation and Assessment:

■ Evaluate students on their use of rhyming words by encouraging them to write short poems using word pairs from their lists.

DAY 5

Activities:

■ Review the story, using some of the variations below.

- Partner reading
- Choral reading
- Reciting from memory
- Small group reading
- Dramatic reading
- Reading with different accents

Enrichment Activities:

Now that all your students can read *Peanut Butter and Jelly,* have some fun with an enrichment activity that goes with the story.

■ Ask students to bring their favorite foods to school.

■ Tape students reading the story and put it in your listening center.

■ Let students write their own innovations by substituting other foods for those in the story.

■ Make peanut butter and jelly sandwiches for a treat! Children may enjoy writing directions for making a peanut butter and jelly sandwich and comparing their recipes with those of their classmates.

■ Hold a peanut butter taste test. Invite children to name their favorite brands of peanut butter and bring samples to class. Blindfold the children as they taste each different sample. Encourage them to describe the taste, write their comments, and rate each brand. Average the ratings to arrive at an overall class favorite. Children may enjoy working in small groups to write advertisements or commercials for their favorite brands.

■ Make your own peanut butter.

SMALL BOOKS

We use small books in two different ways in our classrooms. One way is to read the books in a whole group setting. Each student or pair of students has a copy of the book.. For shorter small books, use the same steps as for big books.

The second way we use small books with our classes is to simply read one or more books to our students every day. We like to choose an author of the week and use his or her books throughout that week.

Use only good stories with your class. Remember those great books you read as a child?

- *The Cat in the Hat* by Dr. Seuss

- *Mike Mulligan and His Steamshovel* by Virginia Lee Burton

- *Are You My Mother?* by P.D. Eastman

- *Crictor* by Tomi Ungerer

- *A Picture for Harold's Room* by Crockett Johnson

- *Amelia Bedelia* by Peggy Parrish

- *It Looked Like Spilt Milk* by Charles G. Shaw

These and many other wonderful books are available as small books in paperback or hardcover. Check them out from your school or public library, buy them from book companies or bookstores, borrow from friends, beg—anything to get enough copies for at least half your class. There is an unlimited number of quality books that are age-appropriate and appealing to the interests of your students. Every story your class reads *can* be a good one!

WRITING INDIVIDUAL SMALL BOOKS

The most popular books in your reading center will be the ones your students have written themselves. A good way for students to begin is to choose a popular big or small book that is predictable and repetitious and to innovate on the text by substituting their own words within the familiar format.

There are two types of books we write with our students. We write individual small books and whole group big books. The individual books are done on a weekly basis and the whole group big books are done only occasionally (every two or three months).

Use the steps below to help every child write a book each week. The children usually work on the books for approximately twenty minutes each day.

DAY 1 — *Format:*

Familiarize your students with a format found in a predictable book or a familiar poem, such as *The House That Jack Built* or "Roses are red, Violets are blue . . ."

Begin brainstorming substitutions for these formats out loud in class and on the board (for your visual learners).

DAY 2 — *"Sloppy Copies":*

Continue brainstorming and have students begin writing their ideas down in rough drafts, or "sloppy copies," while you circulate and conference with children about their content, word choice, audience, punctuation, and spelling.

DAY 3— *Begin Final Copies:*

When students feel that their stories are ready to publish, they may begin transferring their ideas to their final copy. We make final copies by stapling ditto paper inside a piece of 9x12 folded construction paper to form a small booklet. Students begin with the cover, title, copyright and dedication pages.

DAY 4— *Complete Final Copies:*

Students continue transferring ideas from the rough draft copies to their booklets.

DAY 5— *Sharing:*

Allow students to read their completed books aloud to your class and to other classes in your school. Then the students will enjoy taking the books home and sharing them with their families.

WRITING WHOLE GROUP BIG BOOKS

We do whole group big books every two to three months with our students. Each student contributes one page to the book. It may be necessary to work with students in small groups during this time. Here is the procedure we used with *The Chicken Book* by Garth Williams.

After using the book for a week, we asked the children to choose a different character to substitute for the chicken. On their own, they came up with *The Pumpkin Book*. (It happened to be close to Halloween.)

The children each contributed a page to *The Pumpkin Book* by innovating on the text of the passage below.

> Said the first little chicken,
> with a queer little squirm,
> "I wish I could find
> a fat little worm."

We provided the first line for the children by substituting the word *pumpkin* for *chicken* and helped them discover that the last words of the second and fourth lines rhyme. Then the children completed the rhyme by themselves, following the format.

> Said the first little pumpkin,
> _____(rhyme),
> _____
> _____(rhyme).

Not only is *The Pumpkin Book* one of the most popular books in the reading center, but every child can read the entire book! Your students will also love it if you let them make copies of their own to take home. Some of their creations follow.

Said the first little pumpkin
"I don't want to die,
Because I don't want to be
Turned into pumpkin pie." by Melissa

Said the second little pumpkin
"I don't want to be cut,
so I'll go and hide
in a little brown hut." by Noni

Said the third little pumpkin
"I'm afraid of the night
I hope that somebody
Will turn on a light." by Jessica

Said the fourth little pumpkin
"I don't want to be sold
So I'll go hide
In a pot of gold."
by Jong

Said the fifth little pumpkin
"If I sit very tall,
Someone will think
I'm the best pumpkin of all!"
by Aileen

Said the sixth little pumpkin
"I don't want to get hurt,
So I'll go hide
Inside a big church."
By Frank

Said the seventh little pumpkin
sitting on a post,
"I think of all the pumpkins
I must be scared the most."

by Brandi

All the pumpkins got together
and wanted to say,
"Hey you guys, lets
go out and play!"

by Michael

JOURNAL WRITING

Maybe you've tried journals with your class and given up because of all the extra work they involve. We, too, have experienced "Journal Phobia," but we also know that journal writing is too important to abandon without a fight. When children write in journals, they apply independently the skills they have learned through teacher-directed activities. Even more important, they apply them in a non-graded, and therefore non-threatening, situation.

Journals give you an opportunity for informal evaluation on an individual basis. They are a place for children to share private thoughts with you—thoughts they would otherwise never share. Teachers whose students keep journals have a unique opportunity to get to know every one of their students in a special way.

But journals can take lots of extra work. These are some complaints we have heard from teachers.

- Purchased journals are expensive, but putting journals together takes too much time.
- Students just don't want to write in journals every day.
- It takes too much time to reply to every student every day.

We cured our "Journal Phobia" by using these easy suggestions to overcome the negative aspects of journal writing.

- Don't burden yourself with putting together elaborate, expensive journals. Keep them simple. Use spiral-bound notepads or notebook paper in construction paper covers.
- Don't intimidate your students with full-sized paper! They will think they are expected to fill the whole page and be turned off. (Can you blame them?) Use half-size pages and you'll be amazed at the difference.
- Don't get writer's cramp from trying to write back to your students every day. By having journal writing only every other day, you'll limit the number of necessary responses. We only answer each child once a week. You may even choose not to answer them at all. That's okay, too!

Journal writing is a valuable activity that can also be fun. Give our ideas a try. We bet you'll be glad you did!

POETRY

"Poetry! Yuck!" you may say. Well take another look. We have had more fun in our classes with poetry than with any other reading material. Just be sure to select the right type of poetry. Use children's poetry with children! Our two favorite authors of children's poetry are Shel Silverstein and Jack Prelutsky. (See Resources, p. 48.)

Rhyme, rhythm and repetition are the keys to poetry addiction. Remember your favorite "Top 40" song? How many times did you listen to it (and sing it) before you got tired of it?

Steps for using Poetry:

- Once again, select a poem you really like.

- Read the poem aloud to your students.

- Distribute copies of the poem, leaving room for illustrations. (According to the fair-use doctrine, you may reproduce multiple copies of a poem for classroom use.)

- Read the poem again, asking students to join in as they like. Remember, most students join in on the repetitious, predictable parts without any coaxing.

- Next comes an opportunity to be creative. Reread the poem using individual children or groups of children in as many ways as possible. You'll know when your students are ready to go to the next step.

- By now, many children have memorized the poem. This is the time to put the written words away and work on recitation. The children love this part! (Now you're teaching "Public Speaking 101" — remember that course?)

- Performing! Your students will be proud when they memorize a poem. (In order to memorize the poem, they had to read it first!) Let them be performers now — individually or in pairs or groups. They will beg to show off their favorite poem!

- Like Big Books, poems present many opportunities for skill focus. The steps for using Big Books with the whole class will work with poetry, too.

- Reading poetry will inspire your students to write their own poems. Why not capitalize on their enthusiasm by encouraging them to innovate on the text of a poem, write short poems, or work in small groups to create a longer poem.

- Your students may also enjoy reading several poems by the same author and learning about the life of the poet.

AUTHORS and ILLUSTRATORS

Authors and illustrators are real people like you and me. Bring an author to life and you will bring his or her books to life.

- Choose a favorite book. Check out all the books in your library by the same author.

- Introduce the author or illustrator. Make him or her as real as possible. (Share personal information from book jackets and discuss similarities among books, characters, themes, or style.)

- Read the books. Each day, read a book or two to your class.

- Share the books. Make the books available to your students through your reading center. (Get ready — they'll fight over them!)

You'll be amazed! Once you've studied an author or illustrator, his or her name will pop up again and again. Many children's book authors and illustrators share their talents as the table below illustrates.

Illustrator	Book	Author
Arnold Lobel	The Quarreling Book	Charlotte Zolotow
Arnold Lobel	Frog and Toad Together	Arnold Lobel
Arnold Lobel	On the Day Peter Stuyvesant Sailed into Town	Arnold Lobel
Garth Williams	The Chicken Book	Garth Williams
Garth Williams	Do You Know What I'll Do?	Charlotte Zolotow
Maurice Sendak	Where the Wild Things Are	Maurice Sendak
Maurice Sendak	Mr. Rabbit and the Lovely Present	Charlotte Zolotow
Maurice Sendak	Kiss For Little Bear	Else Homelund Minarik
Ezra Jack Keats	Jennie's Hat	Ezra Jack Keats
Ezra Jack Keats	The King's Fountain	Lloyd Alexander
Mercer Mayer	Ah-Choo	Mercer Mayer
Mercer Mayer	The Crack in the Wall	George Mendoza
James Marshall	Yummers	James Marshall
James Marshall	Miss Nelson Is Missing!	Harry Allard
Graeme Base	Jabberwocky	Lewis Carroll
Graeme Base	The Eleventh Hour	Graeme Base
Sami Suomalainen	Mud Puddle	Robert Munsch

READ-ALOUD

The best way to show your students the magic of reading is to model it yourself. What better way to model than to read a good book to your class? The expert on read-aloud, in our opinion, is Jim Trelease. His *New Read-Aloud Handbook* is our classroom bible. His inspiring book is a must for parents and teachers.

■ Here are our ten easy steps:

1. Read aloud to your class *every day.*

2. Read aloud to your class *every day.*

3. Read aloud to your class *every day.*

4. Read aloud to your class *every day.*

5. Read aloud to your class *every day.*

6. Read aloud to your class *every day.*

7. Read aloud to your class *every day.*

8. Read aloud to your class *every day.*

9. Read aloud to your class *every day.*

10. Read aloud to your class *every day.*

■ Some of our all-time favorite books for reading aloud include:

James and the Giant Peach by Roald Dahl. A great starter book for inexperienced listeners — of any age!

Sideways Stories from Wayside School by Louis Sachar. Another terrific starter book.

The Chocolate Touch by Patrick Skene Catling.

The Indian in the Cupboard by Lynne Reid Banks, and its great sequels, *The Return of the Indian* and *The Secret of the Indian.*

How to Eat Fried Worms by Thomas Rockwell.

The Lion, the Witch, and the Wardrobe by C. S. Lewis.

Tales of a Fourth Grade Nothing by Judy Blume and its hilarious sequel, *Superfudge*.

The Black Stallion by Walter Farley.

Stone Fox by John Reynolds Gardiner.

Ramona the Brave by Beverly Cleary and all the books in the Ramona series.

Trumpet of the Swan by E. B. White (the author of *Charlotte's Web*).

Where the Red Fern Grows by Wilson Rawls. (Have a box of tissues ready!)

Snowbound by Harry Mazer.

The Best Christmas Pageant Ever by Barbara Robinson. (Great to read during the holiday season).

Wolf Story by William McCleery.

D. E. A. R.
(Drop Everything And Read)

Set aside some time each day for sustained silent reading. This promotes independent reading skills in your students.

During D.E.A.R. the entire class, including the teacher, reads silently for ten to twenty minutes. (Don't use this time to grade papers. This time is for pleasure reading only!) Let the children choose their own books. Keep an abundance of books in your reading center that your students love to read, such as Big Books, books written by your author of the week, class-made Big Books, and copies of the novel you're reading to the class. Encourage your students to bring their favorite books from home, too.

Some schools do this on a whole-school basis. During D.E.A.R. time, everyone -- janitors, cooks, secretaries, students, and teachers -- drops everything and reads.

ENRICHMENT ACTIVITIES

Any time you can come up with a fun activity that correlates with a story or poem you're reading, you'll be a hit! But don't feel that you have to come up with something wonderful and creative that takes hours of preparation and lots of money. When you no longer need to cram three reading groups into each morning (and feel guilty when you miss one), the fun comes easily—and you'll even have time for it! Remember not to go overboard with extra activities to the point that they take away from the simple enjoyment of reading a book or that you begin to feel pressured.

Here are some enrichment activities we have used successfully.

Chicken Soup With Rice by Maurice Sendak.
   Make chicken soup with rice to eat. (There's also a great album by Carole King called "Really Rosie" that sets the book to music. See Resource List, p. 48.)

"Hungry Mungry" by Shel Silverstein.*
   This poem mentions some strange food. We brought in muenster cheese for our class to try.

"Drinking Fountain" by Marcette Chute.*
   Invite children to choose a common object and think of a way to "perfect" it. Encourage them to draw a picture and write a few sentences to explain their improvements.

Crictor by Tomi Ungerer.
   Compare the use of color in the Crictor illustrations with the use of color in other children's books.

Hansel and Gretel
   Try making a gingerbread house with your class.

The Teeny Weeny Woman by Mary O'Toole.
   Act out the story. You'll be amazed at the different voices and actions your students will come up with.

* MCP *Poetry Works!*

The Little Red Hen
   Make paper bag hen puppets at your
   art center.

The Lion and the Mouse by Mary O'Toole.
   Compare this story with other fables the
   children have read.

The Little Engine That Could by Watty Piper.
   When we read this book, a mom brought
   in a train cake for a class treat.

Jack and the Beanstalk
   Grow bean plants.
   (Hey, that sounds like a science lesson!)

Blueberries For Sal by Robert McCloskey.
   An all-time favorite. Make a blueberry pie.

The Velveteen Rabbit by Margery Williams.
   Have the class bring in their favorite
   stuffed animals.

*Alexander and the Terrible, Horrible,
No-Good, Very Bad Day* by Judith Viorst.
   Write about the worst day of your life.

Miss Nelson Is Missing!
by Harry Allard and James Marshall.
   Make "Miss Nelson" masks.

Miss Nelson is Back by the same
authors.
   A wonderful sequel. Invite your
   principal to read this book to
   your class.

QUESTIONS AND ANSWERS

How do I get started?

Take it slow. Start with one whole-group activity at a time.

How can I have just one reading group when all my children have different oral reading capabilities?

You'll be amazed to find that all your students will read the books together. Oral reading is improved by stories that are repetitious, have natural sounding language, and are predictable. The books we are suggesting have these qualities.

What about all the different skill levels?

By teaching the "grade level" skills through whole group instruction, you will have more time to spend with underachievers in small group instruction. These students should be working at their instructional level with the goal of bringing them up to "grade-level." Many of these students will also be served by Chapter One teachers who provide extra reinforcement.

If I'm using a story (Big Book, small books, etc.) in place of a basal story, how do I ensure that students aren't missing an important skill?

This takes a little planning ahead. Look at the skills that are covered in that section of the basal and emphasize them in the story you are using. You can pull most of the skills from any story. If you find that some stories are better than others for teaching certain skills, make a note of that. Then, the next time you are teaching that skill (perhaps in the next school year), you will already have identified a story that would fit in nicely with the skill lesson.

What provisions do you make for above grade level students?

In our opinion, students should be enriched HORIZONTALLY, not VERTICALLY! It's not necessary to move these students up through a reading series. There are enough alternative ways to enrich those children. Some examples of alternatives are novel reading, critical thinking activities, writing books, reports, or reading to children in lower grades. As a means of communicating their above-average reading ability to their next teacher, however, we do advance above-average and gifted students up through the series.

But won't the children be missing new vocabulary that is introduced in the basal stories?

No. Your students will attain a larger vocabulary through whole group reading and discussion with their peers. If some of the new vocabulary is not covered, you can always use a learning center or a game to reinforce those words. This is another opportunity to use your creativity.

What about skill sheets and activities to go along with the stories?

Don't feel obligated to make worksheets to go with each story. We did just that when we first began whole group reading. Then we realized we were doing just what we disliked about the basal! We were chopping up stories and making skills sheets (creative though they were), for every story. The students hated them. They were detracting from the simple enjoyment of reading the stories. In place of worksheets, why not try some hands-on activities to reinforce skills? (Arrange sentence strips for sequencing, draw pictures for a comprehension check, play a concentration game with vocabulary words, or play win-lose-or-draw using vocabulary words.)

How do you test comprehension and oral reading skills?

Children readily comprehend through whole group reading. The uninterrupted flow of a story is the key to meaning. When a child giggles during a story, he or she must be understanding the humor and therefore be comprehending! Informally, oral reading skills may be checked by listening to children read in small groups or individually.

What about grades and accountability?

As trained professionals, we evaluate children every minute of every day by observing their interactions with both text and peers. We look at group and independent writing, independent use of resources to gain knowledge, and application of reading strategies. Some teachers are still required to take grades from comprehension sheets, workbook pages, or skills practice sheets. Other teachers give a weekly oral reading grade.

What should my lesson plans include?

Lesson plans list the story and skill for each day. Emphasize the skill for the day during reading time by pointing out examples in the story you are using. Expand on that skill during skill focus time. Evaluate the skill before introducing a new one. We're suggesting one or two days for each skill. (See sample lesson plan on page 17.)

How do you find time to use Big Books?

Start by taking just one day off from your scheduled reading groups and do a Big Book through whole group reading. Eventually, when you feel comfortable enough, eliminate reading groups and use Big Books instead. (Aren't your students reading ten times more than they would be in a reading group?) You will still have time left to pull out skills focus groups.

How do you know if every child is participating in whole group reading?

Lack of participation is rarely a problem in whole group reading. However, we all have a "lazy reader" or two. You're more likely to keep a child's attention during whole group reading than when reading basal stories in small groups. The high interest level of whole group reading motivates the usually non-participating child to read with the group.

What if my principal says I must use the basal?

Then use it! But read the stories in their entirety in a whole group setting. You will then find time to use Big Books, too. Another option is to substitute Big Books or small books for some of the basal stories. Remember to apply skills you are teaching as they appear in the stories.

A DAY IN THE LIFE

A DAY IN THE LIFE

Sample Daily Schedule

7:30 - 7:55	Roll call, clerical duties
7:55 - 8:05	D.E.A.R. Time
8:05 - 8:25	Big Books
8:25 - 8:40	Small Books (Author of the Week, small book sets)
8:40 - 9:00	Poetry
9:00 - 9:20	Writing Time
9:20 - 10:25	Lesson Time and Skills Focus Time and Independent Activities: Discuss morning activities and circulate during independent work.
10:25 - 10:55	P.E., Music, Library
10:55 - 11:55	Math
11:55 - 12:20	Lunch
12:20 - 12:30	Bathroom and water break
12:30 - 12:45	Read-Aloud
12:45 - 1:30	Science, Social Studies, Health, Computers, Art
1:30 - 1:45	Read-Aloud and Dismissal

Whole Class Big Books

Your reading group table makes a great plant stand.

Coaches and kids drop everything and READ!

Sharing poetry

Sharing student-made
Big Books

Time to
write

Read!

Read!

Read!

Little Red Hen paper bag
puppets

Hansel and Gretel
gingerbread houses

The Listening
Center

Our principal
reads aloud
<u>Miss Nelson Is
Missing!</u>

Counting to 10 -- OUR Way!

RESOURCES

RESOURCES

Big Book Companies

Modern Curriculum Press, Inc. 13900 Prospect Road, Cleveland, OH 44136. 1-800-321-3106.

Rigby. P.O. Box 797, Crystal Lake, IL 60014. 1-800-822-8661.

Scholastic, Inc. P.O. Box 7501, 2931 E. McCarty Street, Jefferson City, MO 65102. 1-800-325-6149.

The Wright Group. 10949 Technology Place, San Diego, CA 92127. (619) 487-8820.

Small Book Companies

Modern Curriculum Press, Inc. 13900 Prospect Road, Cleveland, OH 44136. 1-800-321-3106.

Scholastic, Inc. P.O. Box 7501, 2931 E. McCarty Street, Jefferson City, MO 65102. 1-800-325-6149.

Troll Book Club. 320 Route 17, Mahwah, NJ 07430.

The Trumpet Club. P.O. Box 604, Holmes, PA 19043.

Weekly Reader Paperback Club. P.O. Box 16628, Columbus, OH 43216.

Professional Books

Anderson, Richard, et al. *Becoming a Nation of Readers: The Report of the Commission on Reading.* The Center for the Study of Reading, 1985.

Cambourne, Brian and Jan Turbill. *Coping with Chaos.* P.E.T.A. Australia, 1987.

Holdaway, Don. *Independence in Reading.* Ashton Scholastic, 1980.

Merrilees, Cindy, and Pamela Haack. *Write on Target.* R.E.A.D. Publications, 1990.

Routman, Regie. *Transitions: From Literature to Literacy.* Heinemann, 1988.

Trelease, Jim. *The New Read-Aloud Handbook.* Penguin, 1989.

Books to Share with Your Children: Big Books, Small Books, and Predictable Books

Alexander, Lloyd. *The King's Fountain.* E.P. Dutton, 1989.

Aliki. *Corn Is Maize.* Harper & Row, Publishers, 1976.

Aliki. *Wild and Woolly Mammoths.* Harper & Row, Publishers, 1983.

Allard, Harry, and James Marshall. *Miss Nelson Is Back.* Houghton Mifflin, 1982.

Allard, Harry. *Miss Nelson Is Missing!* Houghton Mifflin Co., 1987.

Asch, Frank. *Happy Birthday Moon.* Modern Curriculum Press, Inc., 1986.*

Banks, Lynne Reid. *Return of the Indian.* Doubleday & Co., Inc., 1986.

Banks, Lynne Reid. *The Indian in the Cupboard.* Doubleday & Co., Inc., 1985.

Banks, Lynne Reid. *The Secret of the Indian.* Doubleday & Co., Inc., 1989.

Base, Graeme. *The Eleventh Hour.* Harry N. Abrams, Inc., 1990.

Bemelmans, Ludwig. *Madeleine.* Viking Penguin, 1958.

Blume, Judy. *Superfudge.* Dell Publishing Co., Inc., 1981.

Blume, Judy. *Tales of a Fourth Grade Nothing.* Dell Publishing Co., Inc., 1986.

Burton, Virginia Lee. *Mike Mulligan and His Steamshovel.* Houghton Mifflin Co., 1977.

Carle, Eric. *The Mixed-Up Chameleon.* Harper & Row Publishers, Inc., 1988.

Carroll, Lewis. *Jabberwocky.* Modern Curriculum Press, Inc., 1988.

Catling, Patrick Skene. *The Chocolate Touch.* Bantam Books, Inc., 1981.

Cleary, Beverly. *Ramona the Brave.* Dell Publishing Co., Inc., 1984.

Dahl, Roald. *James and the Giant Peach.* Bantam Books, Inc., 1984.

Eastman, Philip. *Are You My Mother?* Beginner Books, 1960.

Farley, Walter. *Black Stallion.* Random House, Inc., 1977.

Five Little Monkeys. Modern Curriculum Press, Inc., 1988.*

Gardiner, John Reynolds. *Stone Fox.* Harper & Row Junior Books, 1983. *

---

* Available from Modern Curriculum Press.

Hansel and Gretel. Putnam Publishing Group, 1981.

House That Jack Built. Playspaces—Internations, 1978.

Jack and the Beanstalk. Putnam Publishing Group, 1981.

Johnson, Crockett. *A Picture for Harold's Room.* Harper & Row, Publishers, 1963.

Keats, Ezra Jack. *Jennie's Hat.* Harper & Row, Publishers, 1985.

Keats, Ezra Jack. *Louie's Search.* Macmillan Publishing Co., Inc., 1989.

Leonard, Marcia. *Goldilocks and the Three Bears.* Modern Curriculum Press, Inc.,1990.*

Lewis, C.S. *The Lion, the Witch, and the Wardrobe.* Macmillan Publishing Co., Inc., 1986.

Little Red Hen, The. Putnam Publishing Group, 1981.

Lobel, Arnold. *Frog and Toad Together.* Harper & Row, Publishers, 1972.

Lobel, Arnold. *On the Day Peter Stuyvesant Sailed into Town.* Harper & Row, Publishers, 1987.

Lobel, Arnold. *Owl at Home.* Harper & Row Junior Books, 1982.

Marshall, James. *Yummers!* Houghton Mifflin Co., 1986.

Martin, Bill. *Brown Bear, Brown Bear, What Do You See?* Henry Holt & Co., 1983.

Mayer, Mercer. *Ah-Choo.* Dial Books for Young Readers, 1976.

Mayer, Mercer. *I Just Forgot.* Western Publishing Co., Inc., 1988.

Mazer, Harry. *Snowbound.* Dell Publishing Co., Inc., 1975.

McCleery, William. *Wolf Story.* Shoe String Press, Inc., 1988.

McCloskey, Robert. *Blueberries for Sal.* Penguin Books, 1976.

Mendoza, George. *The Crack in the Wall and Other Terribly Weird Tales,* Dial Press, 1968.

Minarik, Else. *Kiss for Little Bear.* Harper & Row Junior Books, 1968.

Munsch, Robert. *Love You Forever.* Firefly Books, Ltd., 1990.

Munsch, Robert. *Mud Puddle.* Modern Curriculum Press, Inc., 1986.*

Nelson, JoAnne. *A Home in a Tree.* Modern Curriculum Press, Inc., 1990.*

Nelson, JoAnne. *Peanut Butter and Jelly.* Modern Curriculum Press, Inc., 1989.*

Numeroff, Laura. *If You Give a Mouse a Cookie.* Harper & Row Junior Books, 1985.

O'Toole, Mary. *The Teeny Weeny Woman.* Modern Curriculum Press, Inc., 1988.*

O'Toole, Mary.*The Lion and the Mouse.* Modern Curriculum Press, Inc., 1988.*

Over in the Meadow. Modern Curriculum Press, Inc., 1988.*

Parrish, Peggy. *Amelia Bedelia.* Harper & Row, Publishers, 1960.

Pigdon, Keith, and Marilyn Woolley. *Is There Room for Me?* Modern Curriculum Press, 1988.*

Piper, Watty. *The Little Engine That Could.* Platt & Munk, 1990.

Rawls, Wilson. *Where the Red Fern Grows.* Bantam Books, Inc., 1974.

Robinson, Barbara. *Best Christmas Pageant Ever.* Harper & Row Junior Books, 1988.

Rockwell, Thomas. *How to Eat Fried Worms.* Dell Publishing Co., Inc., 1988.

Sachar, Louis. *Sideways Stories from Wayside School.* Follett Publishing Company, 1978.

Sendak, Maurice. *Chicken Soup with Rice.* Harper & Row Junior Books, 1962.

Sendak, Maurice. *Where the Wild Things Are.* Harper & Row Junior Books, 1988.

Seuss, Dr. *The Cat in the Hat.* Random House, Inc., 1957.

Shaw, Charles G. *It Looked Like Spilt Milk.* Harper & Row Publishers, Inc., 1988.*

Ungerer, Tomi. *Crictor.* Harper & Row Publishers, Inc., 1983.*

Viorst, Judith. *Alexander and the Terrible, Horrible, No Good, Very Bad Day.* Macmillan Publishing Co., Inc., 1987.

White, E. B. *Trumpet of the Swan.* Harper & Row Junior Books, 1973.*

Williams, Garth. *The Chicken Book.* Doubleday, 1990.

Williams, Margery. *The Velveteen Rabbit.* Simon & Schuster, 1983.

Zolotow, Charlotte. *Do You Know What I'll Do?* Harper & Row Junior Books, 1958.

Zolotow, Charlotte. *Mr. Rabbit and the Lovely Present.* Harper & Junior Books, 1977.

Zolotow, Charlotte. *The Quarreling Book.* Harper & Row Junior Books, 1982.

Poetry Books

Cole, William. *Poem Stew.* Harper & Row Publishers, Inc., 1983.*

Greenfield, Eloise. *Honey, I Love.* Harper & Row Publishers, Inc., 1986.*

Hadjusiewicz, Babs. *Poetry Works.* Modern Curriculum Press, Inc., 1990.*

Lobel, Arnold. *The Book of Pigericks.* Harper & Row Publishers, Inc., 1988.*

Moss, Jeff. *The Butterfly Jar.* Random House, Inc., 1989.

Prelutsky, Jack. *Circus.* Greenwillow Books, 1989.

Prelutsky, Jack. *Nightmares: Poems to Trouble Your Sleep.* Greenwillow Books, 1976.

Prelutsky, Jack. *The New Kid on the Block.* Greenwillow Books, 1984.

Silverstein, Shel. *A Light In The Attic.* Harper & Row Publishers, Inc., 1981.

Silverstein, Shel. *Where The Sidewalk Ends.* Harper & Row Publishers, Inc., 1981.

Stories with Music

Burl Ives Sings Little White Duck and Other Children's Favorites. Burl Ives. Columbia
 CC-33183. Includes "The little Engine That Could."

Nelson, JoAnne. *Reading Friends.* Modern Curriculum Press, Inc., 1989.*

Hoffman/Tchaikovsky. *The Story of the Nutcracker.* Claire Bloom. Caedmon CPN 1524.

Prokofiev and Kleinsinger. *Peter and the Wolfe/Tubby the Tuba.* Carol Channing and the
 Cincinnati Pops Orchestra. CP 1623.

Peter, Paul and Mommy. Peter, Paul and Mary. Warner Brothers WS-1785.
 Includes "Boa Constrictor" by Shel Silverstein.

Really Rosie. Carole King. Ode PET-34955.
Includes "One Was Johnny," "Pierre," "Alligators All Around,"and "Chicken Soup With
Rice" by Maurice Sendak.

Record Sources

Caedmon. 1995 Broadway, New York, NY 10023.

Education Record Center, Inc. 1575 Northside Drive, NW, Atlanta, GA 30318-4298.
1- 800-438-1637.

Three Ways to Order More Copies of
Ten Ways to Become a Better Reader

1 Call our toll-free number, **1-800-321-3106**. Have your Visa, MasterCard, or Discover card ready.

2 Fill in your Visa, MasterCard, or Discover card information and mail this form to **Modern Curriculum Press.**

3 Enclose a purchase order or check payable to **Modern Curriculum Press** with this order form and mail it today.

Modern Curriculum Press
13900 Prospect Road
Cleveland, OH 44136

•For further information about MCP books mentioned in *Ten Ways to Become a Better Reader* or other MCP publications, call us toll-free at **1-800-321-3106**.

Order *Ten Ways to Become a Better Reader* (ISBN 0-8136-3485-7)

Name _____

Title _____ **School** _____

Address _____

_____

Telephone _____

☐ Visa
☐ MasterCard
☐ Discover

Please send me _____ copies at $7.95 each = _____

Add 10% for shipping and handling = _____

California residents add local sales tax = _____

Ohio residents add 7% state tax = _____

Total = _____

_____
Cardmember Account Number

_____   _____
Expiration Date   *Signature*